Arcadia

ARCADIA

Christopher Reid

Oxford   New York   Toronto   Melbourne
OXFORD UNIVERSITY PRESS
1979

Oxford University Press, Walton Street, Oxford OX2 6DP

OXFORD LONDON GLASGOW
NEW YORK TORONTO MELBOURNE WELLINGTON
KUALA LUMPUR SINGAPORE JAKARTA HONG KONG TOKYO
DELHI BOMBAY CALCUTTA MADRAS KARACHI
NAIROBI DAR ES SALAAM CAPE TOWN

British Library Cataloguing in Publication Data

Reid, Christopher
   Arcadia.
   I. Title
   821'.9'14   PR6068.E4Z/

   ISBN 0-19-211889-7

*Printed in Great Britain by
The Bowering Press Ltd, Plymouth and London*

CONTENTS

Arcadia	1
A Whole School of Bourgeois Primitives	2
A Valve against Fornication	4
From an Idea by Toulouse-Lautrec	6
The Gardeners	7
Irony and Counterpoint	8
Strange Vibes	9
A Disappointed Bridge	10
Academy of the Aleatoric	11
Pump, Cutlery, Capital P	12
A Holiday from Strict Reality	13
Utopian Farming	15
At Windsor	17
The Man with Big Ideas	18
Big Ideas with Loose Connections	19
Maritime Liverpool	20
Looking Down on the Rich	21
Baldanders	22
The Life of the Mind	23
The Bouncing Boy	24
H. Vernon	25
The Old Soap Opera	26
Low Life	29
Our Commune	31
The Meaning of Morning	33
Ransom and Rescue	35
The Painter and his Friends	37
The Haiku Adapted for Home Use	39
Verge Escapement with Fusee	41
Patience	42
Keelwell's Marmalade	43
In Medias Res	44

ACKNOWLEDGEMENTS

Acknowledgements are due to the editors of the following periodicals in which some of these poems first appeared : *New Statesman, New Review, The Times Literary Supplement, London Magazine*, and *Tuba*.

ARCADIA

In this crayoned dream-town,
the chimneys think smoke
and every house is lovingly
Battenburged with windows.

A studious invention :
these strange, ecstatic folk,
who tower above their dwellings
and whose trees are deckled biscuits,

nuggeted with fruit.
As they step among the traffic,
that lurches down the road
on its long sum of noughts,

they look like damaged packages,
targets for pin limbs,
and yet they contrive to greet us
with smiles like black bananas.

A WHOLE SCHOOL OF
BOURGEOIS PRIMITIVES

Our lawn in stripes, the cat's pyjamas,
rain on a sultry afternoon

and the drenching, mnemonic smell this brings us
surging out of the heart of the garden :

these are the sacraments and luxuries
we could not do without.

Welcome to our peaceable kingdom,
where baby lies down with the tiger-rug

and bumblebees roll over like puppies
inside foxglove-bells . . .

Here is a sofa, hung by chains
from a gaudy awning.

Two puddles take the sun
in ribbon-patterned canvas chairs.

Our television buzzes like a fancy tie,
before the picture appears—

and jockeys in art-deco caps and blouses
caress their anxious horses,

looking as smart as the jacks on playing-cards
and as clever as circus monkeys.

Douanier Rousseau had no need to travel
to paint the jungles of his paradise.

One of his tigers, frightened by a thunder-storm,
waves a tail like a loose dressing-gown cord :

it does not seem to match the coat at all,
but is ringed and might prove dangerous.

A VALVE AGAINST FORNICATION

Biblical families begat, begat . . .
Aunt So-and-so, sprigged out in a prodigal hat,
swoops on the birdie with her eagle eye—
poor, blurred Aunt Sally, one
(and but one) of a claque of maudlin
country-churchyard hens.

Now time has trumped another resurrection
out of this ample ground, where guests
of a wedding wander the graveyard.
We are like broad
sunflowers of empty circumspection,
touched and turned by the everlasting sun.

Deucalion flung this rubble
down on the grass : family headstones,
rolls of the gentry dead.
We pat them on the back, as if they were dogs;
or crouch to read such recondite catalogues :
names in a babel of chiselling, cryptic
runes of the weather, blotting-paper script.

Here is our vicar in his laundered smock,
trying to shake the hands of all his
rambling flock, while Bo-peep
bridesmaids totter round his feet.
We are the famous human Venn diagram, where
two family circles coincide
in bridegroom and bride.
Bells go mad, living so near to heaven.
Speaking with tongues they summon and send us away.

Canapés and circuses, of course!

But why
have all these gentlemen come,
wearing the same disguise, with every
waistcoat-W unbuttoned so,
every top-hat fished from a velvet drum?
Waiters juggle by with trays.
Give me a plate of cataleptic
shrimps on thumbs of buttered bread.

FROM AN IDEA BY TOULOUSE-LAUTREC

Broad beans out of their bath
come to us wrinkled like finger-ends.

They wait on a plate for our solemn
attentions, the ointment of butter.

A syncretic eucharist, supper :
here are two haloes from Denby,

and here, the apparatus
of augury, knives and forks.

Gently, St Laurence does
to a turn in the oven, exuding

incense, garlic and cloves,
the gourmet's odour of sanctity.

Come, let us eat and talk
and be silent together. Our table

is graced by a single chorister—
salt in a fluted surplice.

THE GARDENERS

I love these gardens, all their show
of antiquated art nouveau :
the buxom ironwork, candle-drips
and blobby leafage.
                It is as if
someone had stumbled by surprise
on Alaodin's paradise.

It rains all evening—knives and forks.
The meteors drop by like corks.
Perpetuum mobile, a wind
hums in its box, as gardeners spend
endless, hermetic, twilight hours,
stooping above their hungry flowers.

This is the world's arcanest grove.
The borborygmus of a dove
calls from the belly of its bush.
How carefully the gardeners push
between the clumps of guzzling shrubs,
that line the way in wooden tubs.

With mashing faces, curled-up claws,
most of these blooms are carnivores.
Anyone sees, who wanders here,
a ruby clinging to an ear,
fat fingers, an outlandish wig . . .
The flowers grow slovenly and big,

as gardeners in white linen coats
rotate about their captious throats.
They have a god here, stern and jealous,
wearing four hats and five umbrellas,
who contemplates them, as they strive
to keep strange appetites alive.

7

IRONY AND COUNTERPOINT

Fishtank-lights in the orchestra-pit;
cymbals and high hats anchored like lilies;
black-moth bows . . .

The piano ripples like patent leather.
Somebody brushes sand off his drum,
as trumpets ooze.

The pianist sits and dabs at his keyboard,
as though he were sorting cards for a séance.
Waves of applause . . .

The moon on the floor for a lover to stand in;
microphone perched on one stork leg
with three stiff toes . . .

STRANGE VIBES

That seven-octave smile, those ten
chomping cigars, one with a golden band;

nicotined eyes, and someone's squiggly hookah,
fendered in levers, wheezing the blues;

those three hypodermics pumping in a row;
men groaning and swooning : well, it all went to show

we'd stumbled by chance on an opium-den.
Only the front man kept his cool,

stiff as a waiter and stooping to lay
such infinite knives and forks on a dazzling table.

A DISAPPOINTED BRIDGE

A bleb, a jellyfish, the sun
hung in its watery sky alone.

A foggy reading of foggy matter.
The sea's opaque cartouche gave us

our metaphysics on a platter :
no paradigm and no great perhaps . . .

Only the waves, like brandysnaps,
offered themselves and then were gone.

Winter in a sea-side town
in Yorkshire, with the bookshop shut,

had brought us here along the shore,
collecting marginalia, for

a glimpse of the ES AU ANT, a dog
in full pursuit of a green full-stop,

that stilted pier, bestriding the fog,
but then aposiopetic . . .

Our grey sea and grey sky made one
dismal certificate, stamped by the sun.

ACADEMY OF THE ALEATORIC

The smutty pigeon on a parapet
pecks for crumbs like a sewing-machine.

It gathers all the greys of London,
murky and mottled, into the bunch of its wings.

'Fate looks after the Indian Empire,'
Kipling said, 'because it is

so big and so helpless.' London seems
chock-full of bankers' baroque,

and the clouds save up for some rainy day.
This pigeon is our compendium.

It moves at a waddle from chance to chance,
while the pavement artist broods on his picture.

Tachiste and collage-maker, he knows
that anything goes : scraps and wrappers,

boot-prints, impasto of muck . . .
The dogs and drains append the most delicate touches.

PUMP, CUTLERY, CAPITAL P

Among the logo-bearing lorries
we made our way to heaven,

garage-bunting flagging us off,
and a roundabout redded with poppies . . .

A Whitsun-gift, to be at home
in any new idiom :

words on stilts, triangle-language,
the hieroglyphs at every service-station,

Botticelli and I-Spy !
The fancy packages rumbled by.

You don't have to have been to college
to love an English landscape,

or pick up the aesthetics of road-haulage.
Conical knockabout bollards, trees,

the criss-cross of cat's-cradling pylons,
plotted our horizons.

On holiday, on the M1,
we stopped from time to time

for a cochlear sticky bun,
coffee and a tetrahedron of cream.

A HOLIDAY
FROM STRICT REALITY

Here we are at the bay
of intoxicating discoveries,
where mathematicians
in bathing-trunks and bikinis
sit behind the wheels
of frisky little speedboats
and try out new angles
to the given water.

Everything that we see
in this gilded paradise
is ours to make use of :
palm-trees on the marine drive,
nature's swizzlesticks,
stir the afternoon air
to a sky-blue cocktail
of ozone and dead fish.

All day long
the punctilious white yachts
place their set-squares
against our horizon,
as we lie around on mats
and soak up the heat,
cultivating a sun-peel
that grows like lichen.

A restless volleyball
skips between four figures
like a decimal point,

but the ornamental beach-bum,
who lives under an old boat,
picks at his guitar
and contemplates the plangent
hollow of its navel.

In the hotel bar,
alcoholic maracas
and, on a high glass balcony,
a pompous royal family
of apéritif bottles . . .
Ernesto the barman
tots up a long bill,
castanetting with his tongue.

UTOPIAN FARMING

('Every nation is to be considered
advisedly, and not to provoke them by
any disdain, laughing, contempt or
suchlike, but to use them with prudent
circumspection, with all gentleness,
and courtesy.'
                    Sebastian Cabot : *Ordinances . . .*)

Great maps of dung obliterate the path—
Elizabethan guesswork, or
the aftermath of Ayrshire cows,
come to give milk in the morning.

Real life resumes, as we follow them,
browsing with brooms,
to smudge away these new-found continents,
suds of urinous seas.

Our delicate tubs of fecundity
never quite know which way to go,
hung between legs with swashbuckling,
cream-bag udders, in lieu of rudders.

With kohl-eyed figureheads, beautiful
and dim—if they prance
out of line (manœuvring sideways),
we morris-dance them back as we can.

Meanwhile, the pigs comport
themselves in their sties like Falstaffian
generals, slumped
with buckled muzzles and small, pouched eyes.

We are like sutlers, bringing them water and nuts,
or leaning down to tickle their flanks,
white bristles stiff, as if
from years of soldierly grooming.

Our service seems a kind of a meditation,
and meditation akin to ridicule.
I love to be here, private,
subversive and free, in friendly company,

where pigs on tip-toes
piss with such a haunted look,
you'd swear there was something amiss,
and sleep-walking cattle dump wherever they go.

Hens are galleon-hulled : we take them by storm,
plucking the eggs from under their bodies,
bony and warm—freebooters against
a proud and panicky-wheeling armada.

AT WINDSOR

Farmer Georges all, with heather-
peppered mutton-chops
and gorse-prickled coats, these hunting squires
of London suburbs
have Rovered in with riding-crops,
to keep the Sabbath holy, rubbing
shoulders with famous horses.

This is Arcadian Windsor, home
and stamping-ground
of the Houyhnhnms,
insouciant folk, a cut
perhaps above humans . . .
                              They amble around
in socks and monogrammed beachwear blankets.

A simple toytown countryside,
invented by soldiers, takes the mind
for a comical ride,
lumbering over symbolical fences,
samples of startled hedge, a yellow-brick
wall between nothing and nothing.

Beware the small girl—hair in a bun,
a nippled velvet hat—who can't
control her horse's kicks,
but tackles the oxer with a random,
Pyrrhic plan,
spilling the poles like pick-a-sticks.

Tilting at time, defeated slowly,
her jumper rumbles round the ring.
The other horses stand
about, exhibiting boley
knees and muddy-
clefted rumps and Rowlandsonian curves.

17

THE MAN WITH BIG IDEAS

A framework for another dog,
the whippet, with his shampooed ears
and tail like Hogarth's line of beauty,
stands and fails to watch the hockey.
Rulings, ticks all over the green page
give the game away :
a primitive day,
with schoolgirls straggling at their exercises,
drilled by some shrill pea-whistle.

A group of aimless John-the-Baptists spin
a yellow frisbee from one to another,
their only nimbus, poised like a miracle,
and as full of suspense as a wasp.
'Each part may call the furthest, brother,'
George Herbert said.
—On such a morning, perhaps, of the simplest visions,
when dead leaves bury the dead.

This park is an island ripe for philosophy.
The traffic sounds here no noisier than the sea,
and everything is run on clockwork :
elements of the orrery,
of which we are all some part.
A God-like unity informs creation.
Squirrels proceed by fits of undulation.
Square buses stop by the gate and laugh to themselves.

The whippet's mistress, stuck at the end of her graph,
cuts an almost geometric figure,
with boots, legs, bum, bust
in a top-heavy ziggurat of flesh.

BIG IDEAS WITH LOOSE CONNECTIONS

These monumental Hs must have dropped here
from some heavenly alphabet.

Upright at opposite ends of a turbulent field,
they point woodenly in the direction of hope.

Giants, the epigones of Uranus,
stamp around in the cold, steaming like cattle.

Their lives are ruled by improbable fictions :
lines, flags and whistles;

a thirty-two-legged spider that wheels and buckles
over the agony of its stubborn leather egg.

From a gusty somewhere, God looks down on a world
perfectly simple. We are in love.

The giants are having fun.
Nearby, a blind man tickles the pathway,

whose white stick marks a cardiogram,
no-one but he can follow.

A wriggling, long-tailed kite leaps like a sperm
at the sun, its blurry ovum.

MARITIME LIVERPOOL

The gulls indulge
their crow's-nest fantasies,
stiff-legged mariners
outward-bound.

Plump and fishy
and full of velleity,
they perch on top
of the silliest pinnacles.

Here is a bird
on a king on a horse
on a plinth, who sees
no more than Nelson did.

Fog encircles
the Wallasey ferry :
a gull on the flagpole
has taken command.

A motor-launch,
with its jewellery of tyres,
bobs at the quay
like a harbour tart.

I love these gulls'
uncalled-for heroics,
their swooping down
at the sea and missing it.

LOOKING DOWN ON THE RICH

Stacks of money, the red rock-face
was Arizona's commonplace.

Day after day, the sun patrolled
a Xanadu of crumbling gold :

a zillionaire like Scrooge McDuck . . .
Flying to Vegas, there we struck

what seemed, to foreign eyes, to be
some occult empire of ennui.

Time and again, the ball of fate
ricocheted through thirty-eight

points of the mystic compass. Dice
master-minded our sacrifice,

while madmen rummaged blackjack-cards
for alchemy. Like palace-guards,

the one-armed bandits kept saluting,
or sounded off in spates of shooting,

as visiting generals looked impressed
by the medals that swivel on a manly chest.

BALDANDERS

Pity the poor weightlifter
alone on his catasta,

who carries his pregnant belly
in the hammock of his leotard

like a melon wedged in a shopping-bag . . .
A volatile prima donna,

he flaps his fingernails dry,
then—squat as an armchair—

gropes about the floor
for inspiration, and finds it there.

His Japanese muscularity
resolves to domestic parody.

Glazed, like a mantelpiece frog,
he strains to become

the World Champion (somebody, answer it !)
Human Telephone.

THE LIFE OF THE MIND

Samuel heard the voice of God at night,
but I used to see an Edwardian bicyclist,
a roly-poly man with a walrus moustache.

Since it was always summer, he wore
a blazer with Neapolitan ice-cream stripes,
a yellow boater, made of the crispiest wafer,
and plimsolls, marshmallow-white.

The rules of the game were easy :
to set the man on his bicycle-seat,
and let him balance there, without moving forward.

He never remained for long, and every time
his fall was as terrible as the fall of Eli.

THE BOUNCING BOY

Afflicted at an early age
with Hudibrastic
duck's disease (one gibbous bum
from just below
the shoulder-blades, to just above
the knees); bald, too, from the word go;
fat like a china Buddha; spastic—
even so, he contrived to end up
fairly normal.
           Now he can hardly
remember the time when, stuck on the hulk
of his belly, oblique
to the plane
of things as they truly are—like a Breughel
bumpkin, put down in Cockayne—he nibbled
his Roly Poly Chime Ball, and chewed
the four wheels off his chuff-chuff train.

H. VERNON

The butcher, tired of his bloody work,
has made a metaphysical joke.

Five pigs' heads on a marble counter
leer lopsidedly out of the window

and scare away the passers-by.
The vision is far too heavenly.

With ears like wings, these pallid putti—
hideous symbols of eternal beauty—

relax on parsley and smirk about
their newly-disembodied state.

A van draws up outside. The butcher
opens his glass door like St Peter,

as angels heave in flanks of pork
that are strung with ribs like enormous harps.

THE OLD SOAP OPERA

When Uncle Cecil fled to Europe
with his wicked baggage,
he left behind him,
cluttering the larder,
thirty tins of the golden syrup
he used to sign
into his porridge.
I went to stay with daunting aunts :
three sisters, who shared a wry,
yellow toothbrush,
and read the airmail from my father
in turn
through the plump and glaucous eye
of a magnifying-glass.
(I took this once,
to dazzle Mr Corcoran,
their gardener,
who chased me indoors with a handfork
that bristled with clods and worms.)
They spoke to each other of 'poor Cec'
and 'the devil's handiwork',
but found me an old yapp album,
where, in a blizzard of lace
and swaddled like Captain Scott,
he lay in his mother's arms;
or, naked in a summer hammock,
seemed not to notice the bumblebee
that lit on his forehead
like a benediction.
But there was something odd about the family
and, at his own wedding-reception,
he pretended to be a cuckoo-clock,
which worried Aunt Hester, his bride.
Later, he went swanning off to Biarritz

with a bathing beauty,
bear-hugged a girl in a garden
and dissipated his entire fortune
on prostitutes
in a blustery autumn
of banknotes, jewellery, loose change . . .
On one of his rare visits,
Mr Otterburn, the missionary preacher,
told me that 'the young lassies'
were 'queer fish', and I could see
how he peeled off and pocketed
his awkward wire glasses
in feminine company,
or stepped around
to the safe side of the furniture.
He had travelled
'all over Asia'
and nearly married a princess,
but 'she refused baptism'.
Mr Evans, who fell off a mountain
and now kerb-crawled through town
in a motorized Bath-chair,
took up gadgetry with naïve enthusiasm
and caught his wife and a brigadier
in a burglar-trap of his own invention.
Aunt Hester, I heard,
had plucked the brooch from her bosom
and chased a young girl through a London park,
lunging with the pin and shouting,
'You cow! You cow!'
And I can remember even now
the sweet perfume
of apples left to pucker in a dish
in somebody's dark

and unfrequented dining-room—
a smell I connect somehow
with Cousin Penny, 'snatched away'
by the richest man in Australia.
He kept a retinue
of gloomy servants, guard-dogs
and (his confidant and spy)
a raucous white cockatoo.
The marriage was a failure.

LOW LIFE

These crusty pensioners love to fool
like tiny tots, around
their sunset-citizens' paddling-pool :

obliged to haul about on stumps,
yet strong enough to contend
with mountainous piggybacks on their humps—

such heavy old men of the sea—they slide,
inch by inch, under
the water, as if intent to hide;

or stop awhile and stretch for breath—
each sinewy neck strained
like a marathon-champion's—waiting for death.

But why have all these maundering water-
turtle suddenly turned
up here, in the city's immigrant quarter ?

Who is this cayman, who never blinks ?
And why is the fishmonger's window
heaped with silvery cosh-tailed skinks ?

Ever since the seven Crocodile
brothers were finally drowned
last week in the river—every smile

sewn-up in a well-fed zigzag—things
have been easier. Snakes unwind
all over the floor like ribbons and strings,

or shimmer like livers. Terrapins cram
the sink for days on end . . .
Our pythoness, a one-time femme

fatale, keeps hoisting up her long
plum-stippled lamé stocking, pondering
fine distinctions of right and wrong.

OUR COMMUNE

'A jungle is a machine for climbing,'
somebody said,
and then set up this aluminium plumbing

to prove it. Pipes intersect neatly
overhead,
where most of us lounge and dangle; or sprout directly

out of bare concrete, with angular U-
bends instead
of branches. Very Bauhaus! We make do

with just enough room to swing a monkey,
go to bed
on shelves and indulge in public hanky-panky

like the true Cynics. It could be ideal,
but is it? Dead
bored, a pink-tongued gorilla picks a meal

out of his armpit, reclining as if
at a Roman spread :
his right hand mimes the cigarette that would give him

perfect pleasure . . . Spider-monkeys,
who nurse a dread
of stopping still, play tag on their trapeze

and ignore the puny macaque that hangs
like an old, underfed,
market chicken from one of the exercise-rings.

We study bananas and meditation.
That foul shed
over there houses our guru, the wryly patient

mandrill, whose yellow satyr's beard,
fangs, bright-red
nose and fluted cheeks make him so revered.

Auburn, olive, ashy, white :
every thread
of his coat is remarkable. His hands are folded tight

across his apron, but offer him
a hunk of bread,
and he'll show you his eloquent brown-and-lilac bottom.

THE MEANING OF MORNING

Decision-making at a High Level

Simplicity and opulence :
at nine o'clock, the first tycoon
spread business documents
over a desk,
squares of yellow
for minutes and memos.
There was a bulbous
pouffe like a paperweight . . .
All morning we watched him
pore over bumf
with his brilliant mind,
as the old dog signed
herself into warm spots,
dozed in the in-tray.

The Imperial War Museum

Before us, a morning
of emblems and memories . . .
A squirrel sat on the lawn
like a sketchy fleur-de-lys
on a tattered flag
and trembled as it fed—
a prey to shell-shock
from the autumn bombardment.
Goose-stepping pigeons
pecked about the paving-stones,
where orts of reminiscence
fell from our table,
with its empty tent of toast,
gun-turret of black coffee.

A Coffee-table Book

Matisse's floating world
of nudes and goldfish—
Ah ! if only one
could believe in that.
Here the Sunday papers
do for casual mats.
One grapefruit makes two mandalas.
Your hair is Japanese
with heated rollers.
A floor-mop leans in the corner,
coiffured like a Chinese dragon,
as we flip these pages
celebrating
the marriage of pen and paper.

RANSOM AND RESCUE

Awkward, bluff,
our white ironwork
garden furniture—
Brobdingnag lace—

has reacquired
its sense of place
against these shower-
blackened flagstones.

A winter's evening,
but chairs and a wobbly
table bring back
something of summer :

a pair of glasses,
folded on a book
in lotus position,
that could have dwelt

eternally
on a phrase or two
of mantric print,
while we chattered;

a bumblebee,
like the drunken sexton
at his bellropes,
coming to grips

with a recalcitrant fuschia.
I close the curtains
against the night,
but not before

35

a bus has passed
with its buoyant cargo
of hothouse weather,
gratuitously bright.

THE PAINTER AND HIS FRIENDS

A closed circle :
the intimacy
of pigs in an orange.

Here we sit
around the ancient
ruins of a Stilton,

eating and talking,
drinking and smoking.
A smeared knife

rests on a side-plate
with odd rinds,
to show how the artist

must deal with detail . . .
Somebody's fingers
prise apart

reluctant pigs,
that straggle behind them
strings of white pith,

and one after another
the pips appear
between her lips.

A board of squares,
a bowl of rounds
and our delightful

contiguity
to a check table-cloth
need to be celebrated.

Of course, I relish
the nasal tang
of a ripe Camembert,

the comforting din
inside my head
of a munched apple—

but I shall forget
these trivial things,
once I am painting

my great picture,
The Feast of the Dead.
There, I shall have

a girl in a print dress,
splintering
the skull of a walnut,

to get at its brain.

THE HAIKU ADAPTED FOR HOME USE

I

Ionescoesque,
these pens and papers
have taken over the desk.

II

Water down the drain . . .
I sit, dangling my monocle
from the plug-chain.

III

This carpet is in tatters—
almost like the trail
of a peacock's tail.

IV

Pimpled like lizards,
the gherkins plumb
the depths of their aquarium.

V

A clipper rounds the cape.
Something drops overboard—
of a crescent shape.

VI

A twirly dragonfly
attacks a tin :
it is trying to break in.

VII

The ghosts of spiders lurk among
the fraying curtains
they themselves hung.

VIII

A flying rose
of crumpled paper
lands in my basket, where it grows.

VERGE ESCAPEMENT WITH FUSEE

Ooidal, a chunky gem
for a connoisseur of time!

The infinite kingdom Hamlet
posited, locked in an amulet:

Aleph and abraxas . . .
As though in Chinese boxes,

I picture it safe in the hands
of the German merchant who owned it—

a silver case of fidgety
wheels, rich with activity:

cracked in half like a nut;
squinted into, then shut.

PATIENCE

Our three goldfish
have almost achieved their wish
to be two-dimensional :
part of the watery jigsaw,
they pass the time
quite sublimely.

This kitchen floor
is a great chequer-board,
where only a cook
may jump over the dog,
that lies asleep and barks
at dreams in muted hiccups.

Who constructed
this dangerous Manhattan
of Lego bricks,
which we must not touch—
an afternoon's folly,
monumentally wobbly?

Tick, tock, tick ...
The clock's party-trick
of counting up to infinity
would lead to insanity,
if it weren't for the games
that other objects play.

A competition
of hosepipes and ladders
clutters one end of the garage.
In an empty bedroom,
my mirror says *Snap!*
to the wallpaper opposite.

KEELWELL'S MARMALADE

Outside the station, a cortège of taxis
pursues its business with the personnel of life.

A late-returning milkfloat, bearing prisoners
in metal cages, dwells on a single strenuous note.

The bottles try to keep a common rhythm going—
as vague as hangers in a wardrobe or Aeolian harps,

and totally dispiriting.
A young man picks his way along the High Street.

He notices the marbling where a car
was recently parked,

the fish-shop being swabbed for early closing,
a baby laid to rest in its sumptuous pram.

Because of an absence, he needs to buy a tie.
The gentlemen's outfitter is unusually helpful,

paddling in drawers, repeating soft apologies,
fingering the tape-measure looped around his neck.

Great bolts of cloth are tucked away on ledges
behind him, where they look just as snug as mummies.

IN MEDIAS RES

I

Jerusalem artichokes
with all their warts and spurs,
arthritic ginger-root,

the callused offspring of the earth,
lie on the table between us
ready for paring—

our awkward hands
and the intricate therapy
of knife and water.

II

A pepper with prickles
in a ruddy pot.
A bollard trying to grow a beard.

A balancing-act
of untouchable fruit, stacked
any-old-how by a whim of gravity's.

Your father in the greenhouse
with his watering-can,
cultivating the obstinate metaphors.

III

The weeping willows are dryads
who want to be water-nymphs
and every plunging duck

is a foolish Narcissus.
Nothing that we see
in the park

can quite fend off mythology.
Medea on the tow-path
diverts the birds with erratic crumbs.

IV

A daddy-long-legs
crackles on the wall,
a curious mind investigating corners.

Time undertakes
its wayward enterprise once more,
to find a place of rest.

We cannot sleep :
a dragon above our bed
trampolines upon exiguous hairs.

V

Here at the hospital
for smashed-up old aristocrats
we have finally done away with death.

Our patients—
kings and lion-goddesses,
baboons in their Sunday tippets,

giants without noses—
have taken up Egyptian poses
of infinite expectancy.

VI

With emblematic fishbones
for moustaches,
that feather like rows of oars

whenever they yawn,
the idle-seeming brownies of our house
set to work,

kneading the arms of the sofa
and trussing themselves like poultry,
to clean their hinderparts.

VII

A platitudinous seascape and
a yacht saying *Maybe*
to the wind :

parenthesis between land and land.
Brise marine ...
Our ensign gutters like a candle-flame,

as, not far off,
a dirty tug-boat putters,
sent out to sea to smoke.

VIII

A Sunday-morning hibernation :
your eiderdown protects you
like a tortoise-shell.

My two shoes on the floor
have been abandoned
by their tenants, horrible molluscs.

46

Time to wake up, I think,
to slow kisses
and the snail-life of tongues.

IX
Guddling for soap
in a deep bath,
or trawling a tin basin

with nets of hair—
those small, involving manœuvres—
you hardly notice

how you have caught my attention,
Susanna,
so cruel to the fishy elders.

X
A virtuoso
on his difficult posthorn,
the glass-blower improvises

a molten bubble.
We listen hard,
as, twiddling like a candyfloss-maker,

he modulates
his swaggy bladder
of perilous white-hot silence.

XI

Cigar-box grandiosity :
the pavement we walk on
is sealed with a dozen

fanciful manhole-covers.
The heraldry
of day-to-day :

a cat couchant on bricks;
a baby in a push-chair
blowing a trumpet very loudly.

XII

I am a bishop :
my finger-tips apply
blessings of Polyfilla.

With relics of the true
biblical desert,
we rub the woodwork smooth.

A holy office :
the casting-out of spiders
and anointment with new paint.

XIII

This wooden ship's figurehead
of an operatic contralto
can hardly be heard

above the orchestral wash.
It must be Prospero conducting.
The violinists

are all doing a futile side-stroke.
The brass have held their breath
for far too long.

XIV

Red leather winklepickers,
curly Arabian slippers,
these three chillis

are locked in their jar
like fiery genies.
Safe for now—

but who knows
what revenge they are plotting
against our next intrusion?

XV

Splitting an apple,
I find a cache of commas.
Every tomato

wears an asterisk.
A bookworm in the kitchen,
I take note

how you hold your tea-cup
by the question-mark,
and how you smile in quotes.

XVI

Through a warp in the window
you can sometimes see
the building opposite wobble,

a lorry flicker
like a fish.
Scarabs and bed-bugs—

the impersonal traffic
of a foreign city
moves far below us.

XVII

Caught in a net
of latitudes and longitudes,
the world stands on our table :

imagination.
Dusting a globe
as the sun might,

you turn slowly
and look at me
across a room full of objects.